THE NON-LIBRARY

The Non-Library

Trevor Owen Jones

dead letter office

BABEL Working Group

punctum books ∗ brooklyn, ny

First published in 2013 by
dead letter office, BABEL Working Group
an imprint of punctum books
Brooklyn, New York
http://punctumbooks.com

The BABEL Working Group is a collective and desiring-assemblage of scholar-gypsies with no leaders or followers, no top and no bottom, and only a middle. BABEL roams and stalks the ruins of the post-historical university as a multiplicity, a pack, looking for other roaming packs with which to cohabit and build temporary shelters for intellectual vagabonds. We also take in strays.

ISBN-13: 978-0615945446
ISBN-10: 0615945449

Cover Image: Clougha Egg Cairn (2008), by Richard Shilling.

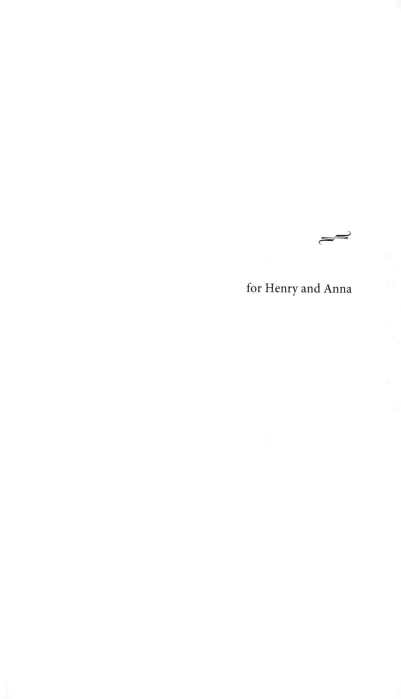

for Henry and Anna

TABLE OF CONTENTS

This is a delirious set-up, but its delirium strictly corresponds to its explosive rigour . . . The theorist says: I am a moral atomic bomb of incomparable power.

Giles Grelet

And every great philosophical text is the gag exhibiting language itself, being-in-language itself as a gigantic loss of memory, as an incurable speech defect.

Giorgio Agamben

The desire for vengeance is a desire for essential equilibrium . . . . The search for equilibrium is bad because it is imaginary.

Simone Weil

In conclusion, by making explicit from the start the primacy of experience (a present practice that could not be replaced by any memory or institution) and the absolute of a goal to be sought after (a final salvation, an ultimate place), they clarified the two terms between which a method could trace a path.

Michel de Certeau

May Heaven forfend that I should ever write a book about books.

> Georg Christoph Lichtenberg

There is no political power without control of the archive, if not of memory.

> Jacques Derrida

I have been forced to become . . . a librarian.

> Georges Bataille

Let us descend now into the blind world . . .

> Dante

01 | Author's Intentions

§1

It is the intention of the author to get away from the discourse of the University, *permanently.*

§2

The Non-Library is, quite simply, the bastardized suspension of the Library as such. This suspension does not perform a taxonomy of operations, but rather is a performance of the immediate and immanent multiplicity the Library itself purports to present. This presentation in turn is not a negation of, say, Borges' Library of Babel; it is its radicality removed from the relief of Quanta. The Non-Library can be discussed through meditations on: 1) refuting the Icon of the Librarian—the guide with bad faith—and instead envisioning a guide along-side us who would access the bolgias of Hell or the vistas of Heaven not for us, but rather with or through us, 2) the Archive, Mnemosyne's vault of treasures and objects that supposedly contains picture-thinking video of "everything that has ever occurred," its instant gratifications waiting for those who would remember, if only properly, and 3) The One—or here, the Real—the harbinger of multiplicity: a multiplicity divorced from Number & its reign (but only absolutely immanently). Effectively, these meditations in turn reveal the Non-Library as a return to a vague understanding that know-ledge is not an object, but a subject. This knowledge comes forth as the Non-Library, the Stranger-in-the-World of heterogeneous (and thus "bastardized") practice, discursive performativity, and textual illumination. To traverse this space, we must call on a Non-Virgil to instruct us, guide us, and perhaps see that the Non-Library is, in fact, the New Library. The Non-Library is where known things are never learned and is here, now.

Drawing on Laruelle, Fichte, Badiou, Bataille, Derrida, Borges, and Dante, the Non-Library pro-poses nothing less than a para-biographical asser-tion of an immanent library as poetic Gnosis for-ever consigned to a silence that is a Joy deeper than any sadness. The difficulty (or, rather, constrained ear-nestness) that arises from an endeavor such as this is simply that one does not explain a mystery by introducing another mystery. To avoid tautology and reductionism, then we simply interrogate the contours of a unidirectional utterance, stylizing itself more as music than as prose, in order to be according to the Real. Or, even better, it's a fitful attempt to bring together that same old dream . . . .

02 | Prolegomena

§1

The Non-Library would be, at first, not the negation of the Library (or a Library) but its suspension of Number, Identity, Soteriology and Memory. What the Library sustains has always been illusion, but in this illusion it has found its material basis in treating information and knowledge in amphiboly. This 'exchange,' this trading, has been the bastardized place wherein the Non-Library returns, but it does not originate from there. Indeed, to speak of origins here is already to corrupt the very careful syntax which we must adopt in order to speak of or conceptualize a Non-Library; this conception must remain immanent to itself, and with that we may introduce an agon that the Library would much rather like to promote as facility. This struggle of the Non-Library to present multiplicity, along with what I call 'classical' suspension, may adequately speak with the Non-Library—that dispersal of shadow inside and outside of Text, texts. The Non-Library is not the 'Great Outdoors' outside of humans' correlation with a nether-realm of noumena, but the dissolution of the grand epic it is to continually consume this 'world' back into 'Spectacle,' description, representation, that Hall of Mirrors that is the Library. Instead, the Non-Library would be a resurrected forest—true, multitudinous, and varied with difference from its extensive quanta. Quanta removed from analysis form into a qualia without subject, however, and in that count-as-one becomes 'Another One.' As Alexander Galloway says, "There are trees in the forest, they are always falling down, and they always make a noise."

This forest we might imagine to be just as judiciously populated with streams of light as pockets of darkness, from ferns and mud to fragmented illumination dashed across limitless foliage. The Non-Library is difference that suspends itself, neither dialectically nor paradoxically.

§2

But enough with these arboreal analogies. I say 'at first' because at first this is merely a dialectical gesture—the adoption of a motif of a certain negative capability would collapse things further still—

the Non-Library doesn't arise in description, doesn't reveal itself in descriptive poiesis whatsoever. To replicate or represent the Non-Library's 'Text' would be to think a conatus which wishes to sustain access or precision back into its subject, but the opposite, or inverse, is not correct either. As for the Library, the reverse is completely the mirrored image of this motion—penetrating or 'gaining' knowledge as information and shedding Light where there is Darkness, settling an instant or object as a oneness or unit to be 'thought,' to progress past that unit of information. Rather, the Non-Library is not a hunger, it is where hunger comes from; access and precision here do not transform dialectically to opacity and fuzziness; instead, they form a triad—access, precision, ambivalence—meaning, simply, the cancellation of a frame that would purport an 'opening' (for whom?) and a surgery, a precise fishing that would pull an 'item' (again, this metonymy to resist) from a collection. The Non-Library might be said to be a 'commentary,' not of particular texts but of 'Text' itself, and also, in that, transcends that mere realm of exegesis, expository, and explanation, which simply pivots back to a relation of *explanans* and requisite *explanandum*.

§3

Illumination is far from the Library's shelves, because William Blake's 'There is No Natural Religion,' sufficiently endowed with its proportion of appropriate irony, points Illumination away. To whom does Illumination belong? Strictly to no one, because there is only Illumination, not the 'Illuminated.' The Library focuses on the Illuminated (which is illusory and, strictly speaking, non-existent), while the Non-Library focuses on Illumination itself.

§4

The Identity of the Library—meaning again, this precision—would propose a 1:1 ratio, a ratio of an item is as to 'I am' as an 'I am.' This is not I=I or another recourse to polyvalent meaning in which some 'perfect reader' simply seizes on the 'correct' meaning; the hermeneutics here delays an espousal, and the communion of 'good news' is instead brought back to its Silence. I say 'brought back,' but the real movement would be nonexistent; the Real, like a mountain, doesn't move 'in search' of knowledge. What would it mean for 'Text' or 'Illumination' to actively find/discover/construct the Real? To go to the Real? The Non-Library discursively purports to disrupt these measures.

§5

At a further removal, that 'Identity' of the Library—its thought to convene, portray and project its knowledge—resurrects that priestly character of mediation, the Librarian. I state resurrection because the Librarian is always imprisoned in a pathetic state of perpetual resurrection. Moreover, that 'bad faith' in which apophatic deduction would only serve to reduce such a figure back to some monstrosity or mote of dust, a 'one' who too readily identifies with clichés of every stripe and letter, who presumes to be a 'guide' through the caverns of Alberto Manguel's *Library at Night*, when in actual fact it is the furthest thing from the case; instead, moral cowardice pronounces taxonomies of access and precision to Global Capital, that 'Google' (the monopoly of monopolies), that glow of letters from a url from beneath a torrent of the forgotten of History, the dead, the victims and every atrocity. Sartre's 'bad waiter' who is too 'waiterly' and the ideologies of the market as knowledge as information convene here to produce this priest who, with their anti-amity and mercenary attitude, does not resolve back to a tertiary figure. We must think alongside this poor figure, and instead find with and through an identity, a 'Non-Virgil'—that hand who trusts and who we trust to traverse the immanence of the Non-Library. This immanence, as Laruelle says, is not absolute but radical. At its 'bottom' (or imagine a knot, or a sphere, or a building, or a statue), at its particularity, this particularity has its own particularity (Borges knew what he was talking about), and this mapping announces a 'peace,' a carefree (but always careful) syntax or discursivity which wonders, "Why all the polemics?" There not being any real exchange, there is no exploitation; there not being any mystery, why wage war? In this case, why then the mercenary of the librarian, the arbiter in the information explosion, a place blown backwards by Benjamin's angel (but all on shifting hedge fund screens, that TV remote toggling from channel to channel). This History, this hallucination, requires exactly that impossible art of oblivion, and in that raising of the Non-Library to the heights of the impossible, it is that lost proximity that comes to a (fleeting) presence. This presence isn't decided on for any exact instant or gesture; it's a dissolution or dispersion across planes. Every ontology is already flat and everyone knows it except the Librarian.

§6

Number, Identity, Soteriology, Memory: this refrain successfully (and successively) brings forth the Library; the Non-Library is that non-thetic Non-Virgil that refuses spatiotemporal metaphor in order to just 'whittle' or cull a thought-item for purchase, sale, possession, hoarding, or reification—there's no exchange with and through the Non-Library, it is a performativity in practice. In sum: we know that someone once discovered water, and we are pretty sure it was not a fish. This would be a non-dialectical stance of rebellion; yes, quietist, but more importantly it is concurrent with the Library's supposed values at any rate. Soteriology? Ok, but also that non-, not as in 'not' or 'anti' but as in non-Euclidean mathematics. Would it define or demarcate a separation loosed from the Library's machinations? Would it travel or carry or labor or speak?

§7

Imagine that Darkness, this Light. Now imagine this Darkness, that Light. This binary toggle switch, this picture-thinking of a candle in a room, this connotation or this 'citation' (the Library is, if anything radically, citation itself) and citation ushers Mnemosyne, supposed monarch of the Muses. Is it of value at all to conjure up the mythos of Memory in its mythological or scientific forms to relegate Memory to war in order to no longer serve the Library? The Library says: whatever is, is saved, is remembered, is recognized. The Non-Library says: whatever is not given will be lost. The excess in the given-without-givenness suspends the Library's all-encompassing Maw of Mater Nacht—that salvation by any means to count the names, to cite the quotation, to connect the dots and hyperlink the plain text, anything to shore this up, take inventory, store away the Pharoah's treasures for use, all this. The excess of forgetting over Memory might be taken to be a travesty, and then dialectically, liberation; as Eco has written, that pure impossibility of *ars oblivionis* is pure impossibility, and separates Being from the Real in that it cannot be traversed, even in artful style (that techne or tool to bring forth, deliver this taxonomy, construct this index). That Baroque fog instead overcomes Mnemosyne, ignores her, ignores that point or punctuation in Time. Time again gives away that Metaphysics the Library insists on, chatters away, mindlessly racing from thought to thought, Title to Title; what is Bibliography but insanity? This source of answer answers in the declarative, announces its poetics of space, its metaphors, to confuse representation of Substance with the Real; it thinks in terms of sentences stating facticity, and then what is interrogation perhaps echoes (again, that embodied spatial thinking). But the interrogative, that question, so phrased (who brings up whylessness, what gives the given)—all these genealogical or originary (patriarchal) idealisms are asking all the wrong questions. Only in a succession of the interrogative—but just the same, without becoming an endless chain of signifiers—can the Non-Library be radically immanent: immanent to nothing.

§8

Theology as analogy; again, another motif, but as Deleuze said, metaphor doesn't exist. Proceeding from the idea of Total Damnation, what would it mean for the Library to record everything? The Archive. *Archive Fever*. Much has been written, for instance, from Pynchon and Beckett, on preterition. Steal away, shrink down, minimize to the invisible—in perdition, damnation, perhaps in Blakean paradox a salvation may be found (or built). Then, with that decision, the Non-Library situates recording, recordedness, access, and precision as so much of a differentiation as to an affront (a hubris?), a petition against solar forces to spare it. If anything, the Non-Library signals a sort of surrender. It spends time with the moon and negative atheologies.

§9

That transcendence implied of the Library, in part
stemming from the transcendental index of the
Library (a sort of catalog or algorithm which dis-
covers or retrieves, 'fetches'), hallucinates or sustains the illusion that it participates in the empirical, it names and demands of the concrete its
movements and cessations, its studious gaze continually mapping a semblance it increasingly 'con-
fuses' with itself, it has metadata to attribute tags
to objects (those definitions always so sound, positive and analytical), able to cut open and apart
(presumably into smaller discretions, descending
and ascending up these ladders of being), and of
course, therefore, an epistemology—a Forgetting
of Being for sure, but also a Forgetting of Forgetting of Knowing. Instead, it is always Knowing! It
deflects the stupor of drunkenness, the gnashing
of the fanatic, and denies any dogma; no, it has the
'pure' knowledge of Physics, the end of Philosophy, the terminus of the Spirit, and only leaves the
management of the world to some questions, and
carries forth with the bad repetition of an unruly,
bad agon which it loves. Instead, the Non-Library
(arriving with Non-Standard thought), says, enough
with that agon. It introduces a more *petit agon*, a
struggle to discover or construct a non-art, a
mode, to perform that gnosis alongside every book
on a shelf or a cache within a server; it is not so
much a rejoinder to the idea of data mining—it
doesn't divide against that antagonism or opposi-
tion, it situates alongside it, embodies that index

or mooring and amplifies in one direction to a volume past its coordinates of measurement or discernability. What would be, in decibels, the sight of the universe blinding itself in an extended modicum of time? Do people ask what is the duration of the flash of lightning behind the mountain?

Here, it is important to remember, against the Library itself: we have positive remembering (sentimentality), negative remembering (history), negative forgetting (repression of trauma), and positive forgetting (liberation).

§10

How does one traverse the Non-Library when it cannot be traversed? That drone, that substrate that provides atmosphere, takes the Library as its material and is the bastardized suspension of the Library. Take genre for instance, or a datum. Sure, anything is susceptible to sabotage. Deception always outruns suspicion they say, but the Non-Library is given-without-givenness, so is a kind of delivery or arrival of terms at once, across a radiant spectrum undifferentiated, propounding differentiation at every turn through its performance. This is not a hermeneutics of suspicion; what presents itself may very well be. It may then, in turn, be incorporated into the Library, with so much plasticity after remembering and after forgetting that remainder, that ananamnesis—if learning is remembering, then forgetting in turn reveals a knowing without ever having learned anything. Such a phenomenon might be know-ledge, but surely isn't information in any cloisters or server farm.

§11

In relation to the ontic or ontological, we might say the Non-Library doesn't wish to point at the something, how something actually is. Indeed, to direct 'at'—this subject-object—belies abstraction: the abstraction chained to that storage in the mind that conjures up the retained as well as the retention. Rather, forgetting aside, against Mem-ory, that abstraction (instead of being drawn out) may simply be doubled or collapsed, but always insisted upon—to get at that abstraction of an abstraction wherein they may change into forms, and as Frank Bidart says, as they change, the forms change and are changed. This superabundance from the empirical, but then relayed into, as Laruelle says, "an example of an example," isn't the Real; it's the foreclosure of the Real. That the Non-Library discusses that gulf from the Library and what it desires, well, there's nothing done (act) or said (discourse-thought) out there that isn't taken up like sand in the wind, all the time.

§12

In short, we can say the Library has its Principle of Sufficient Access and Precision; it wants the Total-ity to be the Absolute. Not only that, but all of this will be readily available and open at all times. The all-encompassing mode of capture and retrieval

the Library wishes to introduce is soundly circum-
vented by its utterly divorced existence. What the
Library wishes to include—the content—has no
predicate. It exists prior to metadatas and taxonomies. It exists prior to descriptive language. It is
poesis, but is not poetry. That wellspring isn't de-
fined against the Library's mode of circular en-
trapment, citation, and "bibliography of God"
Borges proposes in all its sublime horrors. It is
that moral explosion prior to content and form's
scission that shows the multiplicity of 'things' as
they were radically, at root, that Non-Archive
that's not Void. It would be the supersaturation
beyond study, 'knowledge' (modern, positivist
knowledge and objectivity), or Mastery; we might
think of a certain 'epinoia' adjacent to Greco-occidental thought that resists positive definition. This
epinoia of sorts isn't 'inventive consciousness';
rather, it's what makes inventive consciousness
possible. Historically, inventive consciousness has
been born of epinoia, and what has come of it uni-
laterally would be 'the World.' But to say the
World or inventive consciousness has gone back
to this 'epinoia' of a Non-Library of humanity is to
get the cart before the proverbial horse. Again, the
syntax betrays a certain profundity, but only a
profundity that surrounds or envelops its ironies
(which are many) as well; this is the sort of phe-
nomenology, a hyper-phenomenology that must
take its ironies, abstractions, and 'examples of examples' as material into effect, and, effectively,
perform them. Simply, an ahistorical poesis, and
therefore, free.

§13

The Archive: collection, consultation, preserva-
tion, revision. Each visit glosses a document anew.
To steal a glance at something, then to look away,
and to know its fleeting presence is past, was never
there, like moonlight so many microseconds away
always, and to believe this practice constitutes a
'witnessing' of testimonies (so many of them non-
testimonies, so many of them conflicting accounts
of the moral fire that raged through some course
in history). To attribute a 'mentality' on top of the
'primary source,' the agency that burst forth such
verbosity and garrulousness time and time again.
To say 'enough' simply adds to this heap, to this
bonfire, for even these vanities play into the iconodulic function to further valorize the weight of
the past against the living, to weigh down the mass
of what-has-been. That Non-Archive, that conver-
gence, dance and splitting again of potential, possibility, probability, that Future document or letter
of love, that poem, would run neither perpendicu-
lar nor parallel against the Archive (the documen-
tarian's dream), away from the 'witnessing,' to be
suspended from where witnessing's necessity arises to begin with.

§14

The ease of transgressivism: Bataille was quite
clear about banal, simplistic, non-dialectical pre-
sentations or manifestations of the transgressive.
Their terminus does break down to the base, their

resolution is a waste, that secret *Aufhebung*: "someday this living world will pullulate in my dead mouth." People think this quotation is morbid! Let's be very clear: "Authority control" in library science, The Archive as 'order' in *Archive Fever*, these are as open to easy transgressivisms as they appear, and their terminus is precisely that, like water over the side of a vast canyon. These economies come up easily enough with the Library's nomological basis of legitimacy, credibility, authenticity, etc. The conatus of that nomological economy—the violence of the Archive to establish itself, conserve itself, to lash out in wrath and re-establish its museums of cadavers and wounded—this motor or libinidal death-drive cannot be said to issue forth from the Non-Library as 'the first' or the fount of a wellspring; this is precisely the place the Library wishes to command and commence from. Hence, the syntax drops to void (in information science, does not the zero come prior to the count-as-one?). What would it mean to count-as-zero? Does this reinstitute the Non-Library in to so much a vaporous or vanishing mediator of origins? That where the Library or Archive's economics of exploitation and domination reify 'Mastery,' rest assured these machinations do not reciprocally effect the unilateral Non-Library's causations. The Non-Library segues to the Library's follies, but the Library's follies do not fall back into the Non-Library. The Non-Library, as syntactically prior to firstness, appears in negative relation to the Library's surplus or 'base material' garbage; the effluvium of human life, the 'exhaust fumes' and waste from an explosion of information. In turn, that negation, that 'absent effect' from the Non-Library stands alongside the Library's 'effect,' but is not itself effected. Time's arrow goes in one direction: to the future.

§15

On the other hand, the transgressive is hardly what interests or compels a 'telling' of the Non-Library, but its explication and description don't necessarily come to the fore either. To assert the Non-Library as existent is non-sense, as the Non-Library inhabits, with and through, the Library's Decision to Save Everything, the Principle of Sufficient Salvation. Like Laruelle's insistence on the Human to not be qualified with existence or ontology prior to simply the Human, the Non-Library would be the surplus of the Human, the excess of the escape from Language's discourse, psyche's Voice, Technology's wars, Science's Objects and arrival at Reality. This is a departure from Laruelle, insomuch as we might say science is not a monolith, as Badiou equates science with mathematics; mathematics doesn't meet any criteria or 'hanging togetherness' whatsoever as to be a family, a game, etc. Mathematics is not a monolith on the plain; it is dispersed in immanence and grounds nothing. A 'Science of the Human' is just the Human in its abyssal multiplicity; topographically it is as high or deep as a spatiotemporal metaphor allows, and then meets that exhaustion with abstraction on abstraction (which is what poesis is). Pure Quanta isn't 'number' or a counting, and pure Quanta doesn't individuate to a Baroqueness, despite what we think of the beauty that, say, Deleuze brings. Regarding Quanta, as Alexander Galloway said, "there are always trees in the forest, they are always falling, they always make a sound."

§16

The Library's unitary hallucination (say, Alexandria) steep-ed in Greco-occidental thought (to identify and determine any thought whatsoever, to insist on taxonomies, 'an epistemic break,' hierarchies, 'flatness,' networks, mesh, etc., these 'relations' of things and thingness altogether) relies on that pairing and slippage of transcendence and immanence that Laruelle writes of regarding the unitary paradigm in general; 'this' stands in for 'that,' but 'this' isn't 'thisness.' This is to try to raise orchids with a bulldozer. This is synecdoche redoubled, taking the memory for the presence, the crown for the king, but then saying that the Memory itself is the signifier, the crown itself must be revered. These are just making stained-glass windows into bricks for the transgressive iconoclasts, who get recuperated back into this historical circle, the successive cycle (which is infinite) that hallucinates its linear, progressive punctuated equilibriums as a 'spiral,' Yeats's gyre; again, the topographical/spatiotemporal *mixtes* affording themselves professional discipline, reverting back to immanence, then transcendence, etc. The Non-Library is simply without the use of the two parameters, and is only one. It avoids the mixture or mixing, determined already by itself, with and through outside of itself as determining, but not determined. Only a Non-Virgil might walk us through an Inferno and Paradise of zero reciprocity, and then find what follows from this: the potential relations to the Library.

§17

The world's angst over its discretions of analysis and category, its ontologies, meontologies, mereologies, its atomisms and holisms are over with. Instead, the Non-Library introduces a radical ambivalence, asymmetrically divided from the Library's citations, does with its focus on units and unit-making. As the library says "_____," this quotation, this citing of scripture, is always an invocation of the past to determine the present, and worse, to control the future to maintain its equivalence with the past. It presents an economy of stasis of exchange (this happened, ergo, this happens), a punctuation of every instance as event, of every singularity as a particularity carried over to its aggregate. One might accuse the Library of being of the 'cult of experience,' a hallucination of history wrought by the tyrannies of empiricism, even a witnessing, but a witnessing that always fails by its false, deceptive testimonies vying for power. This conservative habit of citation dialectically presupposes pure insurrection, an unleashing of the negative against the status quo; a plastic maneuver, and a priori 'machinic deconstruction,' must insist along with and through this negation an entire map of the Non-Library that cites the future against the past, present, and itself. This is hardly a redeemer or redemption. More simply, it's the auto-position or realization in epistemological terms that there was nothing, or no need, to begin with, in light of redemption. What is remembered and what remembers—both are released from the circle of the Library. To remember an object? To suppose this externality makes a liminal space or a border? However, that is not to suggest the Non-Library allows an easy rebellion; in fact, that is probably the most difficult task in the world. In this, there is much Iconoclasm—movement away from the iconodulic—but it serves its function less reciprocally than it does radically, asymmetrically, apart from one another; rather than a breaking of images to render the pure of heart into the pure desert of the night, it is a breaking of images in the direction life itself ushers forth. It suggests that there is more life in us than what is lived, that there are new icons which defy the vicissitudes of the iconodulisms of capitalism, that the Real thing is as remote and foreclosed as the vague intimacy that saturates, and in this ambivalence, we are already here, now.

Suggesting this presence/absence is to suggest the plenitude of singularities outside the Library's capture, a hyperBorgesian spectrum of the Infinite offering itself as discourse outside of Philosophy's sufficiency; it requires a Non-Virgil of radical amity to traverse this impossible multiplicity, a radical amity that is already immediate. An immediate, immanent, impossible Poesis-without-Logos, without end.

03 | Derrida's Archive

What would it mean to offer commentary on Derrida? Wouldn't this in fact be to rejoin the game, or war, to be more clever than the cleverest Derrida, to be more 'meta,' to construct and execute an irony of ironies on the 'ironist' himself? And for what? To 'best' him, to outflank his maneuvers? Another domination, another deflection of his deflations, to 'deconstruct' the deconstructor? What hasn't been written before about the most writerly of philosophers? And finally, is Derrida not the most 'archival' of all philosophers? Indeed, he is the librarian par excellence. Instead of approaching the text *Archive Fever* in some critical-transcendental mode that we don't in fact possess or inhabit, rather, it would be more demonstrative to animate a gloss with and through Derrida, to simply speak of him, of the Archive, fixate, separate, enhance and engage—but what will be done with the material surveyed at the end?

In *Archive Fever*, Derrida writes,

> *Even in their guardianship or their herme-*
> *neutic tradition, the archives could neither*
> *do without substrate nor without residence .*
> *. . . To conceal itself in a vault or domicile,*
> *this function is archontic and topo-*
> *nomological . . . . Consignation aims to co-*
> *ordinate a single corpus, in a system or a*
> *synchrony in which all the elements articu-*
> *late the unity of an ideal configuration. In*
> *an archive, there should not be any absolute*
> *dissociation, any heterogeneity or secret which*
> *could separate [secernere], or partition, in an*
> *absolute manner. The archontic principle of*
> *the archive is also a principle of consigna-*
> *tion, that is, of gathering together.*

The archive can never dispose of its idealist element of being a mass or unity of collected (consigned) elements. That substrate—pulling together units in a univocal direction—simply posits an extensive set of all sets. And not only that, but that set with a transparent extension which always gives up its content and its syntax (either combination and permutation both belonging to the Archive's glories), this probability, this timeline revealing enough use, reuse, marginal use, and a consultation into its 'depths,' its probity exceeding its magnitude, or what's a heaven for? Humanity has conquered its clutter, its historicity, tamed it and mapped it for exploration and yet more inquiry . . . this syntax betrays the Non-Archive's positive attributes, not in absolute, but in a 'radical' manner it is divorced from gathering—a heterogeneity of dissociation preceding the Archive's elements. The Archive demands a chronological predicate, an 'event' or atomistic incident, instant, or mark; then, its 'museum' hand may arrive invisibly, and so order in a manner of functions a design, a way through the Labyrinth that is already chosen, a foregone conclusion.

Of course, one need not make the Archive a labyrinth at all. What is the Archive if it attends to nuances or fractals of nuances? One would make the argument that the Archive was a totalitarian logic, again setting up an exterior agon against the insistence of Totality as Absolute, but the Archive doesn't even do this. It is more a governance that does not govern, so to speak, a Sovereign without Sovereignty, something that isn't really History but always says it is, and thus, that insurrection, rebellion, etc.

> *This institution of limits from this archive concerns the passage from secret to non-secret, from private to public, what is accessible, rights of publication, rights of reproduction . . . .*

There is something we forgot to mention: the communion of the Secret! Here, with Derrida, it is clear he's on to something. That Library as limit, that very much exhausted storehouse of video, that

Platonic lighthouse filled to the brim with books, that revelation waiting to be revealed . . . this supposes that the confessional—the expository position of regurgitating biographical or prosopographical material as aggregates of individual persons—is not wielding in artifice or invention or creation, but is material to be mined. This atomism splits itself against itself, merely repeating the same thing, then afterwards finding the equivalence of the Library as individuations as part of the whole. Perhaps it really is so much metaphysics, but to our mind, the secret offers real communion more than any telling or Good News ever might. Those individuations at parabolic (non)distance against circumscribed 'knowledge' or record-keeping—the limit demarcates that 'right' or essence into a relationship not merely proprietary, but ontologically devastating retroactively what was, what was in truth and now is something else entirely. The whole celebrates itself and its dominion: always a frieze of slavery, mediocrity, pomposity and contempt.

May the word be so stabilized so as to afford us a monument of its grace? The archive takes place at the breakdown of memory.

When memory breaks down, what occurs? More memory. This cyclical vamping treats silence as though it is pregnant, and not pregnant in the sense of fertile, but of waiting for another lifeless archaeological impulse to bleat itself into and out of existence.

The death drive is not a principle. It even threatens every principality, every archontic primacy, every archival desire. It is what we will call, later on, le mal d'archive, archive fever.

By putting forward the novelty of his discovery, the very one which provokes so much resistance, and first of all in himself, and precisely because its silent vocation is to burn the archive and to incite amnesia, the thing refuting the economic principle of the archive, aiming to ruin the archive as accumulation and capitalization of memory on some substrate and in an exterior place.

. . . the Jew can play the analogous role of relief or economic exoneration (die selbe okonomisch entlastende Rolle) assigned to him by the world of the Aryan ideal. In other words, the radical destruction can again be reinvested in another logic, in the inexhaustible economistic resource of an archive which capitalizes everything, even that which ruins it or radically contests its power: radical evil can be of service, infinite destruction can be reinvested in a theodicy, the devil can also serve to justify-thus is the destination of the Jew in the Aryan ideal.

There would indeed be no archive desire without the radical finitude, without the possibility of a forgetfulness which does not limit itself to repression. Above all, and this is the most serious, beyond or within this simple limit called finiteness or finitude, there is no archive fever without the threat

> of this death drive, this aggression and de-
> struction drive. This threat is in-finite, it
> sweeps away the logic of finitude and the
> simple factual limits, the transcendental aes-
> thetics, one might say, the spatio-temporal
> conditions of conservation. Let us rather say
> that it abuses them. Such an abuse opens the
> ethico-political dimension of the problem.
> There is not one mal d'archive, one limit or
> one suffering of memory among others: en-
> listing the in-finite, archive fever verges on
> radical evil.

Does it bring up an idea of temporality to insist on radical finitude? Not just temporality as a
measure or demarcation within a chronology—a
duration, even—but that idea of this as being
ephemeral. Where then does forgetfulness stem
from? If it is forgetfulness rising above mere repression, it sweeps away "the spatio-temporal
conditions of conservation," that house of memory in which we return to see again 'this' or 'that,'
these single moments or testimonies. Derrida at-
tests that the threat abuses the conditions: "archive
fever verges on radical evil." If the death drive presents itself against the Library as Limit—as negation of the Limit to conserve, possess, and draw
upon—the death drive, *mal d'archive*, destroys it,
explodes it back to its communion as base, and
access becomes foreclosed and remote. With this
negation, but not identified with it, the Non-
Library is against the Limit as absolute because in
it is a priori non-topologically removed from the
Library and its Iconoclasm, the Twilight of the

Archive. The logic of finitude is the Non-Archive set against Derrida's 'Archive,' but also his 'evil' anti-Archive—a countervalence, or double ephemerality: an ephemerality with itself but ephemeral with its own temporality. One could say, "well this is strictly impossible," but what is underscored is that the Non-Library is most definitely not a hauntology. Even with what is haunted or haunting, the sense there indicates that index of reverse dissemination as an art of memory. The art of memory turns useless and decadent at this latitude.

Neither life nor spontaneous memory nor prosthetic experience of the technical substrate, the Non-Library isn't a valorization of forgetting or remembering as such. Some might see this foray as an answer to a question that was never asked, but instead we could reformulate it as the question to an answer that never stops answering and wants everything to be an answer.

> *"Can one imagine an archive without foundation, without substrate, without substance, without subjectile?"*
>
> *". . . and is not the copy of an impression already a sort of archive?"*
>
> *"Freud never managed to form anything that deserves to be called a concept. Neither have we, by the way."*

To avoid impression, but to also dodge or flee its mark by absence, this is the 'New.' The Non-Library is the New Library—the Library not just of the Future, but of an immanence unqualified or mediated apart from itself. This is as much to say that as although the notion or concept (or even the half-formed mutant concept) of 'the Text' may be so much Idealist lather on top of material automations, but to think the constative over the performative may be more the crux in linguistic terms. In 'eidos,' or eidetically, do we care? This is ambivalence, and the metonymy of terms repeats itself again in Plato's nether realm of aery maths. Without a concept conceding to its own self, the Non-Library cannot identify with a demarcation or limit or captured singularity. In the Library (and in other terms, the Archive) everything depends on this relation mattering.

> *If repetition is thus inscribed at the heart of the future to come, one must also import there, in the same stroke, the death drive, the violence of forgetting, superrepression (suppression and repression), the anarchive, in short, the possibility of putting to death the very thing, whatever its name, which carries the law in its tradition: the archon of the archive, the table, what carries the table and who carries the table, the subjectile, the substrate, and the subject of the law.*

With 'law' and nomological *arkhe* arrives transgression. The black angel of Recall devouring a library of videotapes, each labeled and with its corresponding metadata; the Utterly Neutral satanic storm that would reduce 'essence' away, as though humanity's essence were its memories, or that it is condemned to be witness to atrocity, again and again, and so must strike again at atrocity, in external agon (or the pseudo-relation thereof), always committing more war to stop all war. To deny the Library its dialectical 'No' means strictly nothing because the Library already absorbs all this. The Library loves Iconoclasm and renewal as pillage, mutilation, and Year Zeros (or Ground Zeros). Architecture is anarchitecture. The "affirmation of idiomaticity," a certain differing, then deferring, provokes another unity to become "irreducible and necessary." The Library as totality is 'necessary' in order to translate its heterogeneous, 'unique' contents to come to the fore. This double-bind (or amphiboly, as Laruelle discusses it) works either way. The catalog is the actual contents of the library; the library is its catalog. The relation is clear. The ones who survived the burning of Alexandria were the ones who never put anything in it.

One can always dream or speculate around this secret account. Speculation begins there—and belief. But of the secret itself, by definition, there can be no archive. The secret is the very ash of the archive, the place where it no longer even makes sense to say "the very ash." The Secret isn't "outside" the Library, because what would be outside the Library? The Library is taking down notes on everything. It has everything pegged. It smugly smiles when a madman offers another conspiracy theory, when emotions and intellect are delivered on the same plane; the exteriority has to declare itself as Limit, pose a 'naming' to its mathesis of dividing subject/object again. I/Not-I generates the circle back again: the circle with a thousand meanings, etymologies. The flowers of the Good

News are as numerous as they are lovely, and bend toward noon in litanies of color and prisms of light, but for that they can never recuperate their Fortune back to a sufficiency that wouldn't need to document everything; it is all already inert and ready for memory to ruin. The Non-Library isn't 'night' as in the Sun revolving around the Earth (or vice versa). "Black air" accumulates at intervals. The disposal, the waste of 'knowledge,' transcendentally introduces a 'Non-Library,' but this waste precedes economies of subject/object, life/museum, instance/chronosophy; the surplus, the 'gratuitous investment,' syntactically disrupts the 'foundation' of the Library, because it is so radically far away from the foundation of such an institution and all its confusions of metaphor. Derrida's 'death drive' of the Archive reads as a drive, thus, of loss, but the drive comes from the given-without-givenness: a (Non)Text that doesn't need deciphering or ciphering.

Coupling this 'death drive' of absolute forgetting with the Archive's will, how does one establish principles of forgetting, to register its identity against further recording and salvaging, saving? Umberto Eco is very clear about the conditions of the techniques of forgetting: they are impossible. Now, strictly speaking, there is always forgetting, as accident. But what would obscure deliberately? Dialectically, the Archive's order always mutilates its inventory, transforming content, but is this simply another name of forgetting? Quite analytically, through an array of semiotics and presentation of Jakobsonian dyads, Eco concludes artificial aphasia—the cancellation of an icon via an icon—

is impossible. Mnemotechnics is taken as a major bulwark against the creeping nihilism of nominalism, citing 'rigorous relation' and 'real connection' from *signaturae* to *signata*, if not reflecting reality, then at least refracting it. The sign function, the logos and its logico-real limit, demarcate, summon, and propel the chain of signifiers, the associative links which decry homologous relations—an 'interpretative hermeticism' where everything is an icon, an infinite regress as exasperating as it is exhilarating, turning the idiosyncratic subjective relation between two objects or signs founded on historical, logical, mythological data into a grotesque irony in which an anti-nominalism becomes the worst nominalism. If the Library asserts that it is the salvation of every expression and 'real connection' in either dyad or triad, it offers mediation from eminence to the world below; to produce oblivion is the aporia against the Archive's machinations as well its 'exterior' negation, the *mal d'Archive*. This aporia is precisely the beginning of the Non-Library, its introduction occurring not by inducing lacunae into the Library itself—'gaps' as cancellations—but by the multiplication of presences. Whereas 'real connection' is posited as the affront against the onslaught of coming oblivion, 'semiotics' within the Library itself 'stalls natural processes of oblivion.' Instead, what is strictly natural is the Library's hallucinatory fixation of an 'objective reality' set as itself as the perfect mirror within which Historical, Mythological, Social, and Economic reality occurs. The Non-Library is rather a 'real objectivity' with and through the superabundance of signs traversing abstraction removed from a transcendental subject, equivocating fini-tude and processes of the infinite on the same plane so as to afford the most ephemeral, or temporal, flattening (or even [non]-flattening) against any and all ingredients the Library purports. In this, it may be said that the Non-Library is an ahistorical formalism of 'Brazilian logic,' that exploding paraconsistency which allows a 'free for all.' But, in fact, it is not the contradiction which entails everything. (That would be the Library and its Maw of *Mater Nacht*, its gulf of surrounding, coercion, and appropriation.) Whereas ambi-valence may highlight or underscore correspondences from 'both' Text to real or Real to text, this is a dual maneuver always effectively resulting from radical a priori measures of waste, surplus, or excess of multiplicity's measures and self-contained set logic that wishes to define its territories in as many plain languages as possible. Again, this mapping gesture from the Library—its cataloging department, so to speak— promotes or predicates the constative over the performative. While we might say the performative can be constituted over the constative, this in fact would be a contradiction or paradox that isn't helpful. Whereas the constative-performative matrix presents a dialectical pliability (which offers the Library its free range to present facticity, factuality, analysis and its demonstrative 'objective reality,' and the tragico-comic aspects of deranged, facile transgressive insurrectionisms or revolutions to incite themselves), like so many Ming vases on flagstones, we propose 'small arsons' across spasms of silence and constellations of utterance or material superabundance that tectonically shift the Library's foundations while it believes itself to remain unmoved.

04 | Fichte

Less as an act of citation, nor as mimicry, the use of Johann Gottlieb Fichte seems appropriate at this stage. The theurgic quality of any text, all too often ignored or shunned, possesses a great fragility; the attention and focus may pivot away at any moment, the construction of intensity dissipates, disperses. It is my belief that Fichte understood this in his lectures collected in *The Science of Knowing* and in fact drew upon the oral powers of the seminar in order to arrest certain distractions and sophistries pertaining to his project—auto-excluding that which does not belong—and to effectively immanentize, if such a function exists, a spirituality or discourse into a spectrum of qualities, or intervals, deliverable at any moment, but also somewhat opaque simultaneously.

It is an odd remark to those who study (or studied, rather) spontaneous poetics—the now defunct lost cause to a history of the aleatory, the improvisation or invention upon chord changes in modern jazz, etc.—that in a secondary syntax, a spontaneous non-poetics occurs just in time as well. This is less a 'meta' level of mere editing than it is a Real fashioning or construction, a generative approach using language as its medium, but not limiting itself to this happenstance of medium as it occurs.

Fichte. The metonymy of a philosopher's name as an index or substitute to the ideas contained therein of their body of work historically enacted. And so much again, philosophy is really just 'philosophology.' Less as a sterile, academic lens into the generative exercise of sound that is much better portrayed in the works of African-American musicians, Fichte does not bother explicating too much of his historical precedent in Kant but utters his lectures at length and with some repetition, attempting at many intervals the same motion or suggestion. First, as with the discussion of Kant in *The Science of Knowing*, Fichte writes,

> *knowing is a self-sustaining qualitative one-ness that leads to the question, "What is it in this qualitative oneness."*

Fichte concludes,

primordially essential knowing is construc-
tive, thus intrinsically genetic.

What is manifest is factical, and in factical manifestness, an objectivity remains, thus alienated. In
turn, these alien aspects betray the gap, the un-
knowing of its own auto-invention, which Kant
separated as the room for faith, etc. Taking this
manifestness as factical, Fichte says that the world
is facticity, that we are surrounded not just by facticity, but indeed, that the world doubles over its
facticity, its actuality, and its representation or
storied spectacle in the Library as requisite knowledge, so as to better draw on 'the ancients' on the
one hand, or, as Stephen Hawking says, to take
'models' of reality that work and leave the rest to
metaphysical madmen. Without being cheeky, can
one admit this spatiotemporal/epistemological 'gap' is
less of a 'gap' than it is a sublime canyon as wide as
the skies at night devoid of all light?

Fichte's argument notoriously proceeds by steps,
but is quick to beg for understanding from participants.
Indeed, it begs for participation in the lectures
themselves, in the construction of a negation of a
concept by means of manifestness. This manifestness is a self-creation of inconceivability as part
and parcel of the concept it is: its paraconcept.
Fichte calls this the "knowing's inner quality," or
"pure light." Fichte posits one element and dialectically draws upon its annulment. As a third syntactically necessitated maneuver, he orchestrates
the self-genetic mode not as immediate, but as
mediated in a likeness of itself; of course this de-

termination of creativity is mediated as factical after each dialectical turn of the screw.

Fichte wishes to abandon reflection on the content of the material at hand and address the procedure of immediacy given as mediated. This origination, while originally divided, in turn comes to a oneness devoid of any inner disjunction. The "division shows itself to be invalid in an immediate insight." The principle of division is annulled by intrinsic being, he remarks, yet then this being is inconceivable, although to say it 'is' inconceivable is still again to draw upon manifestness for an occurrence which occurs or is occurring as utter self-sufficiency. Fichte admits this is the "sole remaining ground and midpoint—that a radical subjectivity as inner expression of life disengages itself from concept and thereby 'division'"; finally he says, "immediate doing is a dissolving into immanence." This persistence of the immediate as a radical mediation is not lost on Fichte, who declares in the next lecture, "it is clear that it itself stands neither in oneness nor multiplicity, but rather stays persistently between both." While Fichte, as one who is a 'philosopher,' wants to trace multiplicity back to oneness—and it might be said the anti-philosopher or Maoist or Nietzschean may wish for oneness to break into tatters and segments—the analogue, or refusal of discrete unitary selection, is something of a gentle underdetermined sense of the Non-Library's attention to manifestness, the Library's slippage, or verbosity enthralled to Peircean ping-pong balls. The Non-Library's silence offers itself as the midpoint of an immediate mediation, or as a mediated immediacy, but surrendered to a finitude, or phthora ("moral decay"), that relinquishes strength (or any similar attribute) to loss, as it does not take partake in loss.

Obviously Fichte's formalizations and his abstruse German Idealism that was more in conformity with the analyses of his time need not concern us. His schemata, his rules, and indeed his desire for a science of knowing do not exactly fail (although we cannot help but think of what would be of modern philosophy today had Fichte gained more attention than the madman Hegel), yet for all it is worth, Fichte's lectures decry a real aura of the desperate: his predicated communication to others about self-subsistence, about performativity from representation to primary content. This desperation has more than residual affect rhetorically, but focalizes the endurance brought to bear by the "lightning flash behind the mountain," the endurance of the non-manifest through the manifest, the formulation of observation into law, then law to further observation deductively, mixing logics and riffing on participants. The aggregate of such a venture would no doubt come across as very powerful, yet its insistence on the completely original split in light cannot be summoned in a textual sense. The modifications of study, the experience in secondary experience that is "reading" or textual affairs, delving into the Library—all require still more than just: a) a generative syntax of melody, b) secondary negation or editing by auto-exclusion of harmonies, whether following chord changes or sufficing with static harmony, and, to take a musical analog still further, c) the acoustic function in accordance with transcendental terms, not just accounted for a positivistic sense of a perfect composition played on perfect instruments for a perfect listener. A 'musica obvlionialis,' or as Fichte would have it, a finitely posited self with its finitely opposite non-self, would negate its concept in a dialectically temporal second movement, but would reestablish itself along both sides as no difference without a prior unity, and no unity without a prior difference. This emanation of 'light'— all mysticisms that would dare speak their name not withstanding—altogether with immanence, is said by Fichte to be only by proxy; he instills intuition in the service of reason. The Non-Library would only simply reverse reason in service of intuition. He says, "as a consequence of a projection through the cleft or hiatus, the light that does not appear is the graveyard of the concept, it appears in the light that does itself appear." Is this a finite self that projects an infinite self? Whereas before we had decried the Library as a reflection or representation of humanity, is it instead moving toward a Feurbachian projection into terms previously unexplained? This, while no doubt a fertile ground leading to Marxism and which we whole heartedly, amalgamously, take as material for the Non-Library as well, would not take this argument either, as it doesn't properly follow through with the precepts. Therefore, unlike Fichte (and in separation from his otherwise fascinating "trail into the woods of nowhere," which history did not see fit to investigate further, but simply disclosed as another topic for dissertations that no one reads), this is a proposal of an utterly practical, self-transformative performativity in lieu of the pre-scriptions of Voice, Text, Logos, etc., and all that daily violence. To simply dodge daily violence, the stratagems of premeditated spontaneous practice are required, but the disavowal of violence is only an effect of this mediated immediacy; it is only mediated as its immediacy is with, through, and in all things. This ubiquity and invisibility arrive with horror and beauty—two cases in which silence is always the best response and approach.

05: Parabiography

As Badiou remarked of Nietzsche's observation that "philosophy is biography," so too biography must be philosophy: and so, accordingly, 'parabiography.'

The confessional mode betrays itself—it wants to deposit 'all.' It formulates or enhances a format readymade for desire, for desire's determinations in a life lived as foretold, explicated, given 'close reading' and study. Demarcation and declaration are sufficient parameters for reflection, and reflexion—the self-consciousness of a narrative subject that gained its experiences, traversed knowledge, and now possesses the treasure of its object (its object of time as duration folded into unitary discretions of calculation and access). Just so, memory as the bank of karma, trespass, will, and the fundamental aleatory gambits suddenly con-

joined—the impossible rendered compossible—
then runs a full gamut of sensation, ego, factuality,
and the 'cult of experience.' The confessional seeks
refuge from formalization, dissolution, deconstruction, or negation (in the historical mode) by
resorting to its phenomenonological baselines,
beckoning radical subjectivity to the forefront of
that which it wishes to remain solely as back-
ground; the confessional decides its refusal of artifice, despite its apologies for embellishment, exag-
geration, or hallucination (the trifecta that syntactically defines its method), 'desires' a laceration of
affect and a purging to account for the suffering of
the world, then loses itself once again its self-
valorization as declarative, epistemological defen-
siveness. The confessional mode constructs an
archetype of 'quest,' then fails to measure up to its
criteria despite the deafening roar of applause it
hears.

The vindictiveness of confessional, of the Christian pronunciation, resolves into an act of vengeance. Unable to self-lacerate (probably as an encounter with the Real—an actual collision), it lac-
erates against others in an insidious violence that
circumscribes far beyond the realm of the merely
psychical or psychological. While different dis-
courses—scientific or psychoanalytic or therapeu-
tic—have long detailed self-awareness, insight,
behavior modification, and consciousness as do-
mains of legitimate study, their 'mixte' of mental
phenomena against eliminativist quantification
(e.g., brain sciences and cognitive studies) are es-
sentially limited by their positivist outlooks (with
exceptions perhaps being Lacan and some schools

of Buddhist thought). However, even accounting
for the anti-philosophical conundrum, knot, or
koan, we are left with a single-sided (or, as Laruelle says, unifacial) element to bear: the imagined
reciprocity of ego to world, suffering to justice,
truth to doxa. This anticipated binary, while hardly dialectical, remains within the purview of Derrida's art. It lays out the digital physics of yet more
knowledge pointed, or fated, to the Library: the
confessional as glory, autobiography as vengeance,
selfishness masquerading as selflessness. Always, a
"they had it coming" teeth gnashing of Iago in
shadowed alcoves as auto-narration takes shape—
a life confusing its interior with the exterior. This
raises the question of when, if ever, vengeance can
equal justice?

If justice is a sense of universal reciprocity—a
sort of interaction or exchange between the Real
that belies or betrays, say, a cosmic wheel, or
banks of karmic credit and debt that get traded as
daily dividends or derivatives—vengeance is a sin-
gular arrow of time, a unidirectional gesture of
weight thrown in the face of all lightness and its
endless repetitions: a dawn of the idols posing as a
twilight—the weight of not just the 'act,' but the
act's surplus of reality that scorches the Earth ir-
revocably, irreversibily, even with an atonement of
the 'acting out' which the languages of the psyche
attempt to resolve through works, etc. Here, that
wasteful measure (the 'binge' or pure excess of
being that does not equate with the foundational,
originary transgression, but transcends it) destroys
it—in fact so wipes it out that it is erased from
memory—and while Justice is mediated by law

and society, 'vengeance' is individual, a bifurcation of violence at once self-directed and externally wielded. The inverse, of course, would present Justice as existential, suggesting that every life lived desires a primordial balance, a slate free from all obligations and every debt paid to once again radically open all the possibilities which it so deserves; 'vengeance' is the everyday affairs of the State and its institutions. However, it is a blind vengeance which demands satisfaction, and she is in such torpor and in such exhaustion over the ordeal that the satisfaction can never be met, the debt never be paid; the masses mostly only serve the machinations of her Infinite Revenge—that is, to deviate from the constant warfare, or agon, is to further perpetuate the cycle.

Rather, we might meditate instead on the idea of vengeance against vengeance as a resource to draw a line utterly removed from the index of the confessional mode, not just as rhetoric or style but as the false essence it takes itself to be. Revenge contra revenge, vengeance against vengeance, is not a double negation that equivocates to a positive sense, or a mutual cancellation, but rather an emancipatory split, a break wherein memory self-mutilates in order to begin again. And, not just to begin again, but to cease the idea, escape the idea of ever beginning again at all, or to begin with. We notice we don't have to exit the cycle because we never entered into it. This entails a suspension of victimology, or to truly imagine a real victimology without martyrs, or to conjure martyrs but without fashioning them into fixed Icons. This suspension removes itself from generalities, which act as totalities that are always equally and circularly charged, and that are resynthesizing and remixing at every interval and at every curve in the circle, in order to better maintain the circle. The intervals then (less as differends or positive integers counting the progress or success of movements) punctuate a timeliness, a finitude or mortality as radically immanent as non-reference to an object, and while the subject occurs as transcendent (but not transcendental), the changes inherent to a spontaneous channel of non-confessional act on One, with, through, or in One, drawing on multiplicity but not as count-as-one. Count-as-one as a gesture reifies itself as foundational violence, a complacency and recourse to empiricism and correlation that spends itself as an Invisible Icon—an Icon without optics, but an Icon nonetheless. To resist this Icon is less of an effort of withdrawal, but is rather an effort of renewal; this renewal itself is less revelation or salvation and is instead invention, artifice, and poesis. This posits a vision that is less 'pure' than it is purifying. The vision presents itself in radical Quanta, which by definition could be either one or many.

However, we cannot discuss this until later in the chapter on Badiou and Borges. For now, let it remain as intervals of the forgotten who never find their tombs; their tombs are desecrations.

So, finally, as vengeance performs as an arrow in time, and as time as such flows like the arrow in one direction, the 'memory' or 'memorial' of the past need not be vigilantly guarded in order to simply lay it bare and available to all mannerisms of irony, kitsch, etc. Instead, the absolutely unlimited multiplicities of victims in history—who remain faceless, who exactly no one bears witness to or prays for—serve less as some remainders to the processes or algorithms of the historical (the eggs who made the omelettes), but remain in the foreclosed identity of the unknown in open rebellion against the smugness of anything ever justified, still more against the structural revenge enacted on humans simply for living. As Gilles Grelet says, the rebellion, in theory, would then be nothing less than a moral nuclear bomb.

* * *

More in me than I am in myself. Along with me, so that I know I have never been alone, and I 'will have been' never alone, but rather always together with one; I had not seen my friends for quite some time and we were always glad to see one another, always swearing to talk about things but rather, when we got together and drank beers, we bitched about working at the library.

We were standing outside the library on 42nd Street; traffic buzzed and halted around us. Sitting on the steps like the boys and girls in Rome who hang around the Spanish Steps, smoking cigarettes and behaving like the images they see on television (who are modeled after themselves), I think to myself, we are encumbered in one city by Ghostbusters, in fiction parading out before us, haunted in another at the Philadelphia Museum of Art. Citizens, take heed of your cities that hallmark events that never happened, I think. Cosmofiction. I see a stray dog wander by. I flip through the pages of another book or feel the pangs of hangover in my listless brain. Spend the time with the moon, spend more time with the moon, like a witch, I think, listing out things that I'll never do on paper. This stranger walks by; another shadow extends.

We slowly walk to the Mid-Manhattan Library. We walk slowly—the speed of your walk is your freedom indexed. In ancient Greece, my friend tells me you could tell the free from the slaves by their stroll. We whisper through the stacks, catching up on old times, wondering at the inert morasses of our lives before us, not young but certainly not old yet either. Browsing, we think without thinking; not a higher-order thought, but just thought perhaps, thought wherein things come and things go . . . Past tense becomes not even worth worrying about. I remember another line from a film I thought I had invented but was in fact from a real film, only to find out later I had in fact come up with it myself—'Everything's already happened'—but even that suggests a grammar: a grammar I don't care about.

She will go on and on if you let her. She asks me, "Do I name drop?" One could tell all the downtown and uptown bourgeois to stop namedropping celebrities they know—shameless, are they ever called on it? Perhaps like George Bernard Shaw said of horseracing, no, I am not quite sure why people might think it fascinating that one starlet or actress is more or less glamorous than another. These golden pagan bodies, worshipped and falling perpetually. As if all reality has a spectrum disorder now, I think, and we are in the 000s: lists of lists, Guinness Book of World

Records, how-to-be-a-librarians. He chimes in, "we were running, and we still are." In the late '90s and the early 2000s the Internet went bust. Humanities majors found no jobs, and they became librarians. Much of it was a matter of course, predetermined but not in the sense of any fate. I have been forced to become a librarian, the circumstances of which were beyond my control, and I must make, or sculpt, or fashion what I can out of these materials with which I've been given. And yet . . .

Yes, I think. The 100s: philosophy, spirituality. Are there gurus for the dysphoria my friends feel today? We pass through one section, spy at the people on the computers: chess, Facebook, resume, resume, reading the news, resume, email, resume. The rich get richer, the poor can wait for their computer appointments. That was a generation that removed itself from itself. Now they cannot stop burying and enshrining something called *ressentiment*. A server erupts in flames one night, but no one takes notice.

The 300s: politics, political science. We hear a jet overhead. He excuses himself to use the restrooms. She goes to check the catalog for what she doesn't know. Monsoon moon looks like her cuticles, and an archer spelled out in stars brings to mind my own cowardice that I have to live again and again.

Browsing is the art of raising the non-sequitur to the position of narrative. The case being that we only tell ourselves stories, and the anomalies of these stories always provide the irony or tragedy that is there; people are left to pick among the rubble of the remaining plasticity. Of course, we are addicted to telling ourselves stories, but know these are just stories; in effect, we have floating image after image now—not so much that the world embraced the Internet, but that the Internet is now our world, our consciousness. She whispers to me, apropos of nothing, "The spirit is a bone." LOL, and so on.

Table, desk, chair. Laptop, lamp, window. Person, book, book, person. Poetry, health, the 700s, and stadiums of fans adorning each shelf.

Wiseblood: "I know things I ain't never learned." And now today, I think, I learn things I don't know. People get carried off like debris in life if you're not careful. Hold everything dear.

Huston directed the film version. Moral isolation can warp the vocabulary of love into the hideous and beautiful together. The warp and weft, though, can be found in the latter day heart's desire—now externalized and fragmented. A monster you've created, but it is our beautiful monster now.

We are an image from the future. He tells me, the stakes are very high today. A Chinese curse says, "May you live in interesting times." But they are always interesting times, if you tell yourself so. Or at least recognize it. A higher-order thought. And Sartre said, perhaps, by just saying you are dialectical, then you are being dialectical.

Eleanor Roosevelt biography. Baby block books. The Medea Hypothesis. War. Peace. The big things. Eric Satie and small, absurd things: Poincare, cooking, how does one sleep? Africa.

There is contingency in every chance encounter with love and information, which are tantamount to the same thing because knowledge is indexed underneath desire, not scholarship—the contingency appears exactly nowhere in networks with walled gardens and pay-as-you-go pipelines. She tells me all this, first in Spanish, then in Russian, and third in Arabic. People think you ask for the book, then find it, but the truth is the other way around.

Henry Adams thought he could write a history of humanity tethered to the second law of thermodynamics. He was wrong. While we still undergo the slow explosion of history, and physics still remains somewhat legal, there is a lot in between to glance at. A thousand shattered mirrors: the cow in the tornado, Walter Benjamin at the Orange Julius and Dairy Queen, the Dreamtime and people who are no one in particular and the things they love. Random things, in between, and how they happen.

We are done browsing. We checked out some items. I thought I would read some fiction, to keep up with all those Brooklyn literati, I think (I guess). He found a crank title on peak oil and long, sustained emergencies. She will not show me what book she selected, although I suspect its Dewey number. She says goodbye, says her friend said, "The first image he told me about was of three children on a road in Iceland, in 1965. He said that for him it was the image of happiness and also that he had tried several times to link it to other images, but it never worked. He wrote me: one day I'll have to put it all alone at the beginning of a film with a long piece of black leader; if they don't see happiness in the picture, at least they'll see the black." He's dead now.

We say our goodbyes very slowly; everyone on Fifth Avenue hurries on their way to nowhere.

I'm on the subway now. A man in a suit listens to his technology and is flipping through technology. What is on the news today? Some disaster and we will all feel some heavy generic dread? Next to him is a person very visibly without a home; next to him, invisibly, a woman who has been unemployed for several months. A bankrupt student, no way to pay his loans, is sitting across from me, staring at the ceiling, curiously smiling. Wolves, Iceland, meat, flowers, noodles, stars, Sagan, volcanos, barricades and category theory, one after the other, I think; there are dangers in reading, I think, and not all the reading to be done is in books, not all the browsing is done in the stacks, not all things that are lost are the things that are eventually found.

The black space strobes in and out of the car as we all move to the next station, never to speak to one another, floating amidst wreckage and the multiplicities of miscellany.

There I am again, a librarian, working now at a dilapidated downtown library with stately columns in the American South. It is an oddly warm January and I am hauling out stacks of old magazines from the basement. After two days' work the dumpster is full and I'm at a loss as to what to do next. When I was first hired it was not evident what exactly my duties would be, as the library was undergoing renovation after a disgruntled homeless man set it on fire. The building, an old post office from the turn of the century, was only partially damaged, although a number of books burned. When I saw the basement there was a large amount of titles, such as *Atlantic*, *Cosmopolitan*, *Time*, *Sports Illustrated*, sitting on dark shelves—presumably a librarian was saving them for someone to read someday. But the telos of the matter was only me, throwing them into the garbage.

I weeded a large remainder of the law collection as well—all into the trash. I threw out stacks of useless newsprint, yellowed acid paper novels I did not recognize, everything covered in dust and stored for memory in good faith but not faith enough to actually think about what each item's fate might be. No, the only concern for the hoarders of yesteryear was to feel good about themselves such that some posterity, someone wiser, better, more studious, and monied (and thus with more free time, or maybe with a grant's beneficence) would take to the basement and carry the torch of civilization into the blackest of nights. As for me, I didn't think about any of that as the dust rose up; the books cracked open at the spine and when it rained the water returned all the words to an amorphous yellow hulk of pulp.

Confess thyself! Today it is all about individual lives as they are lived, they say. Today we read more biographies than ever because we care more about life than ever, they say. The cult of experience reigns supreme, its insecurities cancerous with open sores of catharsis, breakdown, ellipses, favorites, essences ('essences'), revelations, opinions, pain, enunciation, explanation. The cult of experience brings to bear the cynicism weathering the porticos and alcoves of the Library, that humid creep of rot, the slow torpor that submits all to Ego. It really is all self-interest, each legacy and memorial a tribute to a one, to a 'person.' Indeed, we can imagine a tomb of clay soldiers where one soul equals one statue; each must be accounted for, logged, set, and remain(dered) in place in the basement.

Each extrapolation of an event, each thought taken for an instant inside of duration upon duration, everything and everyone can be saved in time. With enough time, the Library will be the encounter that explains, but doesn't produce. It sits inert while it imagines its constant work and diligence to corral atrophy, to stave off entropy, to bring to light what is threatened by darkness, and nothing is worse than book burning, etc., etc. Of course, not all biblioclasms take place under the aegis of fire and its comfortable recognition as antagonist or Anti-Christ. Dialectically, the summation of arson is tantamount to the negation of the Library's answers: its encyclopedia places knowledge under arrest, and absorbs itself into the very same unit as the confessional. Confess, and sins will be absolved! We wish to speak of another fire . . . a fire in the Non-Library would be that encounter which doesn't explain, but produces. It would be an encounter not mediated by time or the experience of a subject (which is radically open as a frozen plain)—it instantiates an agoraphobia of sorts metaphorically. Of course, agoraphobia is something of a misnomer; whereas the agora or market would be teeming with people and business, this is more akin to the claustrophobia and 'racing thoughts' of the Library, the Archive full of Biography! Every little life, stored away, neat and on the shelf—no, rather a kind of massive horizon, windswept and achingly deserted; this sheerness, this blankness, lives with more life than may actually be lived, spilling out across one another and without proper synecdoche.

A droning doesn't repeat itself; it is the same unit, sustained, and dissolves those metrics by its persistence or force. This force is a radical suspension of the chattering Library's mediocre proximity, always within conversational or amicable distance. The Non-Library, on the other hand, as a harsh flatness in difficult circumstances, invokes an intensity, an intimacy much nearer to a face. The face is the Stranger in the world: the original face. This closeness is immediate and is a guiding hand traversing an unwieldy cosmos foreclosed to thought. As Zen masters used to say, "What is your original face? Who is the Stranger in the world?" This radical You-ness (not as in Ego or psyche or higher-order thought theory), cross-referenced to void, picks up on something that is akin to the Non-Library's existence. More like a droning, removed or withdrawn from a listener or an ideal listener, than some ideal reader at midnight, absorbing all texts—it subtracts, and doesn't negate, time and spatial analogies and crutches. We'd say, well an existence without consciousness, what the heck does that mean? An irony that swallows its tail. An existence without ontology? Tongue-in-cheek and thousand-yard stare. Let us approach the mountain . . .

06: Borges, Badiou, Bataille

Far from composing yet another critico-trans-cendental critique of Borges' "The Library of Ba-bel," as though interpretation would somehow 'unlock' or explain it, Borges' relation of the Li-brary may be sutured to Badiou's famed project of wedding set theory to philosophy, and yet again, under-determined by Bataille's warrant of excess and more importantly, his secretions of vulgarity and decomposition into a heterogeneous synthesis without resolution. This 'mixte' again draws best in the fashion of the Library to call forth its cita-tions, explicate their intentions, master the heretofore unsaid art involved, and declare once again another argument in favor of this or that. In a rigorously political stance then, the Non-Library establishes a radical cut to this, imposing a non-anagogical brief throughout an otherwise straightforward expository.

There is a city at a crossroads of war. Mutual armies meet headlong outside its walls, blackening the sky here, brightening it to blood-orange with the fury of bombs and explosives there. The fields outside are salted, and refugees have flocked to the gates. The masses inside are starving and take to collective self-improvisation to distribute foodstuffs to the needy, and all the while matrices of heroes, scoundrels, opportunists, and adventurer types gather to discuss seizing power and ending the crisis. A monk in black robes immolates himself and the poor wooden throne he sits on, burning without moving. The classes of schoolchildren scurry in fright. The statesman's entourage bullies its way through the remains of the bazaar, taking prisoners and commandeering the last supplies of grain for the barracks. Storm clouds pregnant with thunder and rain hover above the citadel for days, failing to wash out the fires from the unending siege, and the philosopher-king deep inside the keep has long ago committed suicide; the statesman and his entourage keep the suicide a secret, not wishing to induce panic through the citizenry, let alone the constabulary. From the jailhouse, one Promethean hisses and swears unholy revenge on the city should his revolt manage to issue from the gray monochrome walls. Further afield, amid a congregation of makeshift shacks and huts, the

Church and the Library sit listlessly. The scholars have all joined rank with the statesman's perpetual emergency, and the schoolteachers have had their protests to save the insides of the Library from the random arsons occurring every night. Every artist and mystic in the bazaar is concerned, but careful not to chiefly attend to the Library's welfare lest they betray their uselessness to the military's growing conscriptions. On the forty-fifth day, a riot breaks out in the animal stalls over malnourished pigs; the rain begins, but the fires have made their oily slick across the sky with machines and the Library faces its end . . .

A blind man, an old man, and a drunk sit across the plaza. It is rumored the blind man is a reactionary, that he incessantly adopts a kind of dumb purity which no one expects, yet he always runs further afield masquerading in the name of something or other. Because he is blind, no one has ever called him a fool. Yet . . .

The old man is a windbag. Known for lengthy bombasts of farts, prognostications and prescriptive politics for the young (who cannot be bothered as they are too busy being young), the old man has a small group of adherents in the plaza who imagine themselves revolutionaries. While the ruthless statesman and his colluders daily execute those in their path (and in as cynical fashion as possible), the revolutionaries talk themselves into circles and attempt to hyperventilate over how things "should be" in the city. One of them elopes to take up arms with the blacksmiths' guild, and in turn is murdered and lies in an unmarked grave.

The drunkard, one cannot help but feel, was once a man of some worldliness, of some kind of wisdom. However, there is also the unmistakable whiff of "everything that can happen with this man has already happened." He had gone to see the elephants and speaks of evil, madness, and spiders; his sentences give others pause, but their meaning is unclear. It is said he is a drunkard, that he is a layabout, a little man in a black peacoat, although no one sees him drink, no one actually catches him fornicating. But his reputation precedes him nonetheless.

The blind man sat while the Library burned (and it is always burning): "I have imagined a Library beyond imagination. I have like Joyce scripted a text that demands yet defies interrogation for the ages; I have fashioned a correspondence that dances across the mind in flights of numerosity. I have devised an eternity of returns and each secret incorruptible with them, but I have also punctuated this effort with a sort of cessation, of a sort of certainty that is aroused in poets' minds that betrays a naïve arrogance: the Library's production of Languages required for each and every inquisition, the 'interpolations of every book in all books,' the infinite consultations and speculative perversity, the aesthetic delirium. However, I did say, 'To speak is to fall into tautology,' so perhaps I am not such a fool . . . ."

The old man, just having undergone a very severe bout of flatulence, spoke up, "Blind man, who has held beheld Aleph can ever consider 'eternal return' ever again? Think of cardinality. Every series of number may have its terminus, but that ter-

minus equals only the archi-transcendent character of the One marked by zero. I myself discovered
a new Platonism to unify Void with multiple, to
exhibit zero throughout plenitude, and in demonstration after demonstration I said the cardinali-
ties are infinite, that the infinites are infinite, that
we are Immortals who, as Non-Pythagoreans, con-
join the political as urgently ontic against Being's
separation from Number, but instead, rejoice! I
speak of militancy that is everywhere and nowhere; the world must be changed through Ideas. I
offer a prescription so that militants may have
more than just recourse to . . . handing out meal
tickets." The old man had puffed up his chest, and
his acolytes clapped. The Library continued to
burn.

The drunk had had a poor day. He did not
know why, but he still appeared every day for
work, despite the crisis. He was desperately hung-
over—the kind of hangover that spills a sickness
metaphysical from the pores of the skin. He felt his
loathsome brain in his head like the mushy bug-
organ that it was. The clamor of the world half-
hooded his eyes as though at all the times, indeed
even for most of his existence, he had desired
nothing more than to sleep; he had concocted a
Lotus-eating together with several of his lovers
that defiled the most obnoxious of Nietzschean-
isms down to niceties boastful and silly. His spine
bent crooked over his frame as he shuffled
through the smoke and business of the plaza, away
from the applause and the incessant prophesying
from blindmen, madmen, blueballed would-be
heroes, glassy-eyed fanatics, the bored satirists, the

cynical shoppers, the misanthrophic homeless. The Library was burning now and in one door the drunk fetched up from the basement a single manuscript and said nothing to no one. In twenty-four hours the battle was over, but the ashes of each hexagon plied against one another in desperate cross-reference from the other librarians who attempted to reconstruct the precious histories of the kingdom. In the final night of victory over the besiegers (or perhaps the besiegers had won, no one was sure), the Dionysian sorts rioted again, turning over cars and lighting bonfires. More books were accidentally burned. It is not known if the drunk had saved just one book, or a few; in fact, it is not known the fate of him or any of it. In a week the Library was rebuilt, restocked, and re-arranged. The blind man kept writing poetry. The old man kept farting and calling for militancy. The drunk was nowhere to be found.

More philosophology. But what of music?

07: Meditations

The introduction of the heart

At the heart of all things,

The radical center,

The Stillness that Is, the Mountains & pale naked sky.

The introduction of self to self, of rude

Awakening

To music without sound, force,

Without words.

The drone.

The radical center, and its emanate,

Its emanate in amity; a story always

Contains sadness.

The Library catalogs each story and names it.

It has its anthropology of the name,

but rather it makes a taxonomy

Of the human divine. Less divine than really

Everyday Life,

The survival of the meek, the ones

In flight or taking refuge light their

Fires in the evening across the valley floor.

The snow has muted

Every inch of the kingdom this evening.

The lights, the torches, do not flare

Up one-by-by but rather all

At once;

Simultaneous full floral fires

From the peasants in rebellion

When the moon is covered.

Not individual or collective

But egalitarian in its amphiboly, not and

And and

But the beyond of conjunction.

Imagine the lost books of antiquity

Restored, memorized and recited to their development,

Their waxing as organic and natural;

The counterhistories only sprout up as obscenity

To the reality of injustice. The hauntology

Evoked by a murmur, a photograph,

The Cheese in the Worms,

Every morning No-Mind to the

Original face, just sitting.

Movement of sadness slipping along signifiers,

Hart Crane threw himself overboard,

Albert Ayler went to drown

In the East River.

❧❧❧

The torture of the Library

Continues. The Non-Library, not antagonist

But antidote, dwells at rest

In a location not far from

You or your friends. It is

Waiting and

Is the sound of the river

As you are sitting attending,

Every Icon celebrating its end,

The mother twilight song

Gathers every wolf to

The bonfire, the Unnatural

And the Natural ignoring what

Has been made the law by the Wise and

The Good. The Wise and the Good

Know nothing of stupor or evil, and for that

We can be thankful,

For in the stupor and the evil of the

Bonfire's light, the Iconoclasm

Inherent across the span of God, of

I don't believe in God,

I believe in something much larger,

That Silence of the meadow

And the empty city

And the contours

To know

The city by moonlight,

To spend time with the moon,

To dash the Sun,

Or the Sun as every instance

Of Being and Appearing

Together,

At the Radical Center

Between experiment from

The cult of experience's dogma

To the fools' skepticism

Every performance an exception

To the endurance of time and existence

Pronounced neither one nor as many

Nor as explanation,

Between experiment as a bridge

From the unknown to the know, just

So many answers in search of questions or

Interrogation seeking

Its victim,

An experiment housed

In the gesture from the known

To the unknown, of

Speech that says enough and says

No more. To take leave

Of the philosopher-kings,

The poets' profundity,

The Ironies of the Library,

The radical non-sequitur

Across its host

In the night to not properly

Explain mystery but to

Be according to mystery where (No)

Hand guides you save Love

Unbound, unconditioned

From the predicates of suffocation

That every Archive screams through,

The Christians demanding every

Witch to come forth to daylight, the caul

Removed from the babes' heads and hacked to death,

The genocides every church establishes, for every

Deterritorialization a reterritorialization,

And for this one

Enacted together

Submit the rebellion

Of peasant fires across

Time, the ultimatum of not only survival

But Joy inhabiting

The interior and exterior, the variance of

Amplitude or intensity without distinguishing

Save one from count-as-one, the Bomb of

Non-Violence, the biblioclasm against

The Word of God and the

Non-Book never written. The Space out of Time or

Time out of Space, that grayness

Depicting twilight liminality which

Asks nothing in exchange but

As occurrence of the Impossible,

In sweet knowing, a closeness to the present,

Who I asked to stay with me but will not,

Who I prayed would return,

Who I demand self-sufficiency,

Who what will be the Future,

The intermediate fire that services

As intercession of Void and fullness in

One volume at the drone

Of the bottom of the world,

The bottom of the world in banality

Married with Abstraction's Queen,

Abstraction's Queen beholden to Memory,

The Imperfect Perfection delimiting my dreams from

My failures as they are recounted,

The continuous vastness as microcosm

Inherent or parasitic of the Soul

As Nothing across one shape, two shapes, or

Many, every geometry another approximation

To the circumference.

In me more than myself, the Workers

Composite against the coming storm falling

Across the walls of the city, the trees

In shock from their slumber,

The drunken waste of a reactionary foregoing

His dreams and he who cannot

Sleep, the eyes of the madman

Leading Terror to the fray;

Every personage or permutation located

In the frame cannot submit to the

Frame, the parameters of a mathesis

Articulated in a sphere of noise to

The steps of the Library and its holdings. To

Make for the desert, to suppose an

Intelligibility strike or an

Apophatic atheology

As communication as in

Communion, *communitas*

Demands of us the activity or

The exercise to suspend

Human suffering,

Finally.

The non-consistency

Of a practice against the Library, to

Introduce a simplicity of

Identity in the last instance,

To accord knowledge accordingly,

All things through, with and in

The Heart at the Heart of all things,

Which takes up itself

And crashes into the sea

To renew the world without renewing,

To inaugurate the New Library,

The New Life,

The radical center of a human

Bursting from its captivity

Because it must

Without question,

Without answer.

08: The Non-Virgil

The Non-Library is radically opposed to the growth of the Library. Opposed not as in antagonistic, but a resistance opposite the existence of this model called the Library. François Laruelle, in "The Degrowth of Philosophy," offers non-standard terms to understand negative ecologies in the same sense as there are negative philosophies—the Non-Library is immanence under-determined and 'oriented' to degrowth. This orientation includes: 1) the suspension of Number (Quanta removed from unitary discretion); 2) Identity in the naming of taxonomies and hierarchies; 3) Soteriology in the anagogic sense (in which every Library illustrates every Heaven); and 4) Memory—the bourgeois-sentimental synecdoche of history and human consciousness which is constantly confused and hallucinated next to the Real, or, the self-narration of every life lived as egography as opposed to biography, which is merely the episodic chartering of things that happen to a subject. This 'confessional mode,' with its idiotic violence and the saber rattling of 'storytelling' is the outcome of poets' misplaced ambitions worn thin through crisis after crisis. Such is Memory as supposed Muse). The Library, as the network or marketplace of information, experience, and gnosis, monetizes 'energy' back into horrors of reification much as Marx has written about—the struggle of the Non-Library to maintain its heart at the threshold of the One and Many with its 'classical' suspension of the authority of texts over human beings. As Fichte argues, this isn't to exit the correlation of consciousness with reality, but to draw down the power to continue to add to the 'growth' of the Library. The principle of Sufficient Information, which the Library always finds fit to catalog, describe, and circulate, is suspended for the Non-Library.

Dante's *Inferno* as an allegorical reading of life as a prison, as a labyrinth requiring traversal without turning around, draws on the work and the figure of the Roman poet Virgil to accompany the poet into the depths of hell—*The Divine Comedy* in turn, as a whole, suggests a teleology from beginning to end in its linear composition to eventual *Paradiso*, "the timelessness of the celestial rose." Virgil, of course, does not go with Dante into Heaven, and instead stays put on the wheel of inferno and purgatory—while Dante is the pilgrim or the son, Virgil is the guide or the father. While perhaps Dante's intent on not bringing the pagan Virgil into Christian Paradise is obvious, it also explains Virgil's fatalistic exclusion of telos against cyclical returns, repetitions of differends without end, only requiring a Stoic, Roman sensibility to endure it. If the Non-Library is a radical diagonal across the spans of the Library, a Non-Virgil as a guide for praxis again portrays accompaniment and ordeal together as an 'amity' constructed in the cosmic-epic sense. This concept, while fixated on Virgil in the *Inferno*, simply takes the representation as its material and uses it according to the precepts of non-standard thought.

Access and precision are not afforded in the depths of the Library, or Non-Inferno. The surrendering of will to the outside only demands the radical self-fashioning compossible with amity (or, Love); if every unit through Babel astronomically eradicates a thought, divides it, every book accounted for, every permutation of every alphabet considered, the Non-Library simply precedes alphabets: a sequence of symbols to list this, describe that, control one function, order one person from another. The Non-Library functions as an illiteracy gained after the dialectic, after deconstruction, from the Spectacle's dream and the Library's conspiracy.

Taking on a 'hyperseriousness,' the Non-Library incorporates humor; taking on the fecundity of the universe in a much more sincere manner than the Library's mimicries and imitations, its sickly clones are usually left without light, oxygen, or water. Illumination, as "There is No natural Religion," save for what occurs in transcendent features of immanence afforded to itself, activity autoindexed and thereby foreclosed to study.

With the Non-Virgil, as he extends his hand, it is not that there is nothing that can be said; it is more that nothing will be.

References

Adams, Henry. *The Education of Henry Adams.* New York: Library of America Paperback Classics, 2009.

Agamben, Giorgio. *Means Without End: Notes on Politics.* Minnesota: University of Minnesota Press, 2000.

Alighieri, Dante. *The Divine Comedy.* New York: Randhom House, 1995.

Allouch, Jean. *132 bon mots avec Jacques Lacan.* Toulouse, France: Éres, 2000.

Ayler, Albert. *Holy Ghost.* Austin, Texas: Revenant Records, 2004. CD.

Badiou, Alain. *Being and Event*, trans. Oliver Feltham. New York: Bloomsbury Academic, 2007.

Badiou, Alain. *Ethics: An Essay on the Understanding of Evil*, trans. Peter Hallward. London: Verso, 2013.

Bataille, Georges. *The Accursed Share, Volumes II and III: The History of Eroticism and Sover-*

eignty, trans. Robert Hurley. Cambridge, Mass.: Zone Books, 1993.

Beckett, Samuel. *Molloy*. New York: Grove Press, 1995.

Benjamin, Walter. *Illuminations: Essays and Reflections*, ed. Hannah Arendt, trans. Harry Zohn. New York: Schocken, 1999.

Berger, John. *Hold Everything Dear*. New York: Vintage International, 2008.

Bidart, Frank. *Desire: Poems*. New York: Farrar, Straus and Giroux, 1999.

Blake, William. *The Complete Poetry and Prose of William Blake*. New York: Anchor, 1997.

Borges, Jorge Luis. *Labyrinths: Selected Stories and Other Writings*. New York: New Directions, 2007.

Browning, Robert. *Robert Browning's Poetry*, eds. James F. Loucks and Andrew M. Stauffer. New York: W.W. Norton & Company, 2007.

Certeau, Michel de. *The Mystic Fable: The Sixteenth and Seventeenth Centuries*, trans. Michael B. Smith. Chicago: University of Chicago Press, 1995.

Crane, Hart. *The Complete Poems of Hart Crane*, ed. Marc Simon. New York: W.W. Norton & Company, 2001.

Deleuze, Gilles and Guattari, Felix. *Anti-Oedipus: Capitalism & Schizophrenia,* trans. Robert Hurley, Mark Seem, and Helen Lane. New York: Penguin Classics, 2009.

Derrida, Jacques. *Archive Fever: A Freudian Impression*, trans. Eric Prenowitz. Chicago: University of Chicago Press, 1998.

Eco, Umberto. "An Ars Oblivionalis? Forget It!" PMLA 103.3 (May, 1988): 254–261.

Fichte, Johann Gottlieb. *The Science of Knowing: J.G. Fichte's 1804 Lectures on the Wissenschaftlesre*, trans. Walter E. Wright. Albany, New York: State University of New York Press, 2005.

Galloway, Alexander. *French Theory Today*. New York: The Public School New York/Erudio Editions, 2011.

Ginzburg, Carlo. *The Cheese and the Worms: the Cosmos of a Sixteenth Century Miller*, trans. John and Anne Tedeschi. Baltimore: John Hopkins University Press, 1992.

Grelet, Gilles. *Déclarer la gnose: D'une guerre qui revient a la culture*. Paris, France: L'Harmattan, 2002.

Hawking, Stephen. *The Grand Design*. New York: Bantam, 2012.

Laruelle, Francois. *From Decision to Heresy: Experiments in Non-Standard Thought*, ed. Robin Mackay. Falmouth, UK: Urbanomic/Sequence Press, 2013.

Laruelle, Francois. *Philosophies of Difference: A Critical Introduction to Non-Philosophy*, trans. Rocco Gangle. New York: Continuum, 2011.

Lichtenberg, Georg Christoph. *The Waste Books*. New York: NYRB Classics, 2000.

McMurtry, Larry. *Walter Benjamin at the Dairy Queen*. New York: Simon and Schuster, 2001.

Meillassoux, Quentin. *After Finitude: An Essay on the Necessity of Contingency*, trans. Ray Brassier. New York: Bloomsbury Academic, 2009.

Manguel, Alberto. *The Library at Night*. New Haven: Yale University Press, 2009.

Masciandaro, Nicola. "On Commentary." Public Lecture delivered for The Public School New York, Proetus Gowanus: An Interdisciplinary Gallery and Reading Room, Brooklyn, New York, May 19, 2011.

O'Connor, Flannery. *Wise Blood*. New York: Farar, Straus and Giroux, 2007.

Peirce, Charles S. *The Philosophical Writings of Peirce*. Mineola: Dover Publications, 2011.

Pynchon, Thomas. *Gravity's Rainbow*. New York: Penguin Classics, 2009.

Sans Soleil. Dir. Chris Marker. Criterion Collections, 2007. DVD.

Sartre, Jean Paul. *Critique of Dialectical Reason,* Vol. 1, trans. Quintin Hoare. London: Verso, 2004.

Shakespeare, William. *Othello*. New York: Simon & Schuster, 2004.

Vonnegut, Karl. *Mother Night*. New York: Dial Press, 1999.

Weil, Simone. *Gravity and Grace,* trans. Emma Crawford and Mario von der Ruhr. New York: Routledge, 2002.

Wunderli, Richard. *Peasant Fires*. Bloomington, Indiana: Indiana University Press, 1992.

W. dreams, like Phaedrus, of an army of thinker-friends, thinker-lovers. He dreams of a thought-army, a thought-pack, which would storm the philosophical Houses of Parliament. He dreams of Tartars from the philosophical steppes, of thought-barbarians, thought-outsiders. What distance would shine in their eyes!

~Lars Iyer

www.babelworkinggroup.org

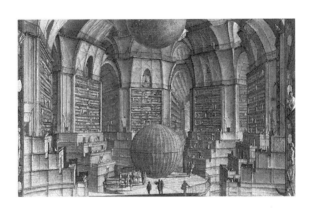

I HAVE BEEN FORCED

TO BECOME ... A LIBRARIAN

.

Made in the USA
Charleston, SC
14 March 2014